Resolutions and Advice to Young Converts

Resolutions and Advice to Young Converts

Annotated

Jonathan Edwards

Waymark Books

Copyright © 2024 by Waymark Books

This is a proofread and newly designed edition of a public domain work.

CONTENTS

INTRODUCTION TO THE 70 RESOLUTIONS vii

1 | The 70 Resolutions 1

2 | Advice to Young Converts 16

ABOUT JONATHAN EDWARDS 27

INTRODUCTION TO THE 70 RESOLUTIONS

A conscientious regard to duty appeared greatly in the early as well as in the latter days of Jonathan Edwards. As a child, the spirit of love and obedience uniformly guided him; and as a pupil, he discovered every disposition honorable to himself, encouraging to those who anxiously watched over his progress, and which was justly considered as the earnest of uncommon attainments. The child, the youth, the man, all presented to view the same superior mind, in different degrees of advancement, but still alike indicative of the same general excellencies.

While at college, he paid a most assiduous and successful attention to his assigned duties, and particularly to the study of mental and physical philosophy; yet he still found time for pursuits of a more elevated and spiritual character. His whole education from early infancy, and the counsels of his parents, as well as his own feelings, prompted him to these pursuits. "To read the Bible daily, and to read it in connexion with other religious books, diligently and attentively, on the sabbath, was made, in the earlier days of New England, the habitual duty of every child; and his father's family, though not inattentive

INTRODUCTION TO THE 70 RESOLUTIONS

to the due cultivation of mind and manners, had lost none of the strictness, or conscientiousness, which characterized the pilgrims. The books which he found in his father's house, the conversation of ministers often resorting to the house, the custom of the times, as well as the more immediate influence of parental instruction and example, naturally prompted a mind like his to the early contemplation and investigation of many of the truths and principles of theology. He had also witnessed in his father's congregation, before his admission to college, several extensive revivals of religion; and in two of them the impressions made on his own mind had been unusually deep and solemn. The name familiarly given by the plain people of New England to these events--"A religious attention," and " A general attention to religion"--indicates their nature; and those personally acquainted with them need not be informed, that during their progress, the great truths of religion, as taught in the Scriptures, and as explained in the writings of theologians, become the objects of general and intense interest, and of close practical study; or that the knowledge, acquired by a whole people at such a time, in a comparatively little period, often exceeds the acquisitions of many previous years. With all these things in view, it is not surprising, that, to these two kinds of reading, he devoted himself early, with great diligence and with great success."

Two of his early "Resolutions" relate to this subject, in which he proposes "to study the Scriptures so steadily, constantly, and frequently, as that I may find and plainly perceive myself to grow in the knowledge of the same." He never lost sight of this resolution. On the 8th of June, 1723, he also proposes, whenever he finds himself in a dull, listless frame, to read over his own "Remarks and Reflections of a Religious Nature," in order to quicken him in his duty. These "Remarks and Reflections" were very numerous. The first manuscript of his "Miscellanies" is in folio, and consists of forty-four sheets of foolscap, written separately, and stitched together. When he began the work, he had obviously no suspicion of the size to which it was to grow, nor had he formed his ultimate plan of arrangement. He headed his first article, "Of Holiness;" and having finished it, and drawn a line of separation across the page, he commenced the second, "Of Christ's mediation and satisfaction." The same is done with the third and fourth. The fifth he writes, without a line of separation, in larger letters, "Spiritual Happiness." After that the subject of each new article is printed, or written, in larger letters. His first article was written on the second page of a loose sheet of paper; and having written over the second, third, and fourth pages, he went back to the first. He began to number his articles by the letters of the alphabet, a, b, c, and having gone through, he commenced with a double alphabet, aa, bb, cc; when this was finished, finding his work enlarge, he took the regular numbers, 1, 2, 3, &c. and this plan, both as to subjects and numbers, is afterwards continued.

The beginning of the work is written in a remarkably small round hand, nearly the same with that in which his earliest productions are written. This extends through about the first 150 articles, and is soon after perceptibly changed, into a hand somewhat more formed and flowing. These appear obviously to have been written during the last years of his college life, and the two years of his residence at college as Bachelor of Arts. Large extracts from this work will be found in the present edition of his Works, and a number of them from the earlier articles. Such are the Miscellaneous Observations, and the Miscellaneous Remarks, vol. ii. page 459. and the Miscellanies, page 525. In these will be found many of his most original and most profound thoughts and discussions on theological subjects.

"His regular and diligent study of the sacred Scriptures, led him early to discover, that they opened before him an almost boundless field of investigation and inquiry. Some passages he found to be incorrectly rendered; many were very obscure, and difficult in explanation; in many there were apparent inconsistencies and contradictions; many had been long employed, as proofs of doctrines and principles, to which they had no possible reference; the words and phrases, as well as the sentiments and narratives, on one part, he saw illustrated, and interpreted those of another. The Old Testament, in its language, history, doctrines, and worship, in its allusions to manners and customs, in its prophecies, types, and images, he perceived to be introductory and explanatory of the New; while the New, by presenting the full completion of the whole plan and design of their common Author, unfolded the real drift and bearing of every part of the Old. Regarding the sacred volume with the highest veneration, he appears to have resolved, while a member of college, that he would, as far as possible, possess himself, in every part of it which he read, of the true meaning of its Author. With this view he commenced his "Notes on the Scriptures;" obviously making it his standing rule, to study every passage which he read which presented the least difficulty to his own mind, or which he had known to be regarded as difficult by others, until such difficulty was satisfactorily removed. The result of his investigations he regularly, and at the time, committed to writing; at first in separate half-sheets, folded in 4to; but having found the inconvenience of this in his other juvenile writings, he soon formed small pamphlets of sheets, which were ultimately made into volumes. A few of the articles, to the number of about fifty, appear to have been written while he was in college; the rest, while preparing for the ministry, and during his subsequent life. That he had no suspicion when he began of the size to which the work would grow, is plain, and whether he afterwards formed the design of publishing it, as an illustration of the more difficult and obscure passages of the Bible, perhaps cannot be determined with certainty. A few of the articles of an historical or mythological nature, are marked as quotations from the writings of others, and are omitted in the present edition of his Works. The reader, after perusing the work, will be satisfied that they are the fruit of his own investigations; and that his mode of removing difficulties was,--not as it too often is, by disguising or misstating them, but by giving them their full force, and meeting them with fair argument. Perhaps no collection of notes on the Scriptures so entirely original can be found. From the number prefixed to each article, it will be found easy to select those which were the result of his early labours. Such a plan of investigating and explaining the difficulties of the sacred volume, at so early a period of life, was probably never formed in any other instance, and evinces a maturity of intellectual and moral attainments, not often paralleled. Among the most interesting and able of these investigations, will be found the discussion of the sacrifice of the daughter of Jephtha, Judg. xi. 29-40.; and that on the principle advanced by Paul, in Romans viii. 28. That all things work together for good to them that love God; which as being contained in his letter to Mr. Gillespie, of Sept. 4, 1747, is omitted in the notes on the Scriptures."

The class of which Edwards was a member, finished their regular collegiate course, in Sept. 1720, before he was seventeen years of age. At that period, and for a long time afterwards, the only exercise, except the Latin Theses, given at the public commencement, to the class of Bachelors, was the Salutatory, which was also a Valedictory, Oration in Latin. This exercise was awarded to Edwards, as sustaining the highest rank as a scholar among the members of the class.

He resided at college nearly two years after he took his first degree, preparing himself for the work of the ministry; after which, having passed the customary trials, he received a licence to preach: this was in the nineteenth year of his age. In consequence of an application from a number of ministers in New England, who were intrusted to act in behalf of the presbyterians in New York, he went to that city in the beginning of August, 1722, and preached there with great acceptance, about eight months. While there he found a most happy residence in the house of a Mrs. Smith; whom, as well as her son Mr. John Smith, he regarded as persons of uncommon piety and purity of life, and with whom he formed an intimate christian friendship. There also he found a considerable number of persons, among the members of that church, exhibiting the same character; with whom he enjoyed, in a high degree, all the pleasures and advantages of christian intercourse. His personal attachment to them became strong; and their interest in him as a man and a preacher was such, that they warmly solicited him to remain with them for life. To decline their candid invitation was most distressing to his feelings; but on account of the smallness of that congregation, and some peculiar difficulties which attended it, he did not think there was a rational prospect of usefulness and comfort. After a most painful parting with the kind friends, under whose hospitable roof he had so long and happily resided, he left the city on Friday, the 26th of April, by water, and reached his father's house on Wednesday, the 1st of May. Here he spent the summer in close study, during which he was again earnestly requested, by the congregation in New York, to return to that city, and settle among them; but his former views were not altered; and therefore, though strongly inclined from his own feelings to gratify them, he could not comply with their wishes. Probably in no part of his life had he higher advantage for spiritual contemplation and enjoyment, than in the period first mentioned. He went to New York in a delightful frame of mind. He found there a little flock of Christ, constrained from a sense of their own weakness to "dwell together in unity," and to feel a practical sense of their dependence on God. He was in the midst of a family, whose daily influence served only to refresh and to sanctify. He had also much leisure for religious reading, meditation, and prayer. In these circumstances the presence of the Comforter appears to have been a daily reality; the evidence of which he found in that purity of heart which enables its possessor to see God, in the peace which passeth all understanding, and the joy with which a stranger intermeddleth not.

During his preparation for the ministry, his residence in New York, and his subsequent residence in his father's house, he formed a series of resolutions, to the number of seventy, intended obviously for himself alone, to regulate his own heart and life, but fitted also, from their christian simplicity and spiritual-mindedness, to be eminently useful to others. Of these the first thirty-four [6] were written before Dec. 18, 1722, the time in which his Diary, as it now exists, commences. The particular time and occasion of making many of the rest, will be found in that most interesting narrative, in which also are many other rules and resolutions, intended for the regulation of his own affections, of perhaps equal excellence. It should be remembered they were all written before he was twenty years of age. As he was wholly averse to all profession and ostentation; and as these resolutions themselves were plainly intended for no other eye than his own, except the eye that is omniscient; they may be justly considered as the basis of his conduct and character, the plan by which he governed the secret as well as the publick actions of his life. As such they will deeply interest the reader, not only as they unfold the inmost mind of their author, but as they also show, in a manner most striking and convincing to the conscience, what is the true foundation of great and distinguished excellence.

He was too well acquainted with human weakness and

frailty, even where the intentions are most sincere, to enter on any resolutions rashly, or from a reliance on his own strength. He therefore in the outset looked to God for aid, who alone can afford success in the use of the best means, and in the intended accomplishment of the best purposes. This he places at the head of all his other important rules, that his whole dependence was on the grace of God, while he still proposes to recur to a frequent and serious perusal of them, in order that they might become the habitual directory of his life.

The 70 Resolutions

"Being sensible that I am unable to do anything without God's help, I do humbly entreat him, by his grace, to enable me to keep these Resolutions, so far as they are agreeable to his will, for Christ's sake.

Remember to read over these Resolutions once a week.

1. Resolved, That I will do whatsoever I think to be most to the glory of God, and my own good, profit, and pleasure, in the whole of my duration; without any consideration of the time, whether now, or never so many myriads of ages hence. Resolved, to do whatever I think to be my duty, and most for the good and advantage of mankind in general. Resolved, so to do, whatever difficulties I meet with, how many soever, and how great soever.

2. Resolved, To be continually endeavoring to find out

some new contrivance and invention to promote the forementioned things.

3. Resolved, If ever I shall fall and grow dull, so as to neglect to keep any part of these Resolutions, to repent of all I can remember, when I come to myself again.

4. Resolved, Never to do any manner of thing, whether in soul or body, less or more, but what tends to the glory of God, nor be, nor suffer it, if I can possibly avoid it.

5. Resolved, Never to lose one moment of time, but to improve it in the most profitable way I possibly can.

6. Resolved, To live with all my might, while I do live.

7. Resolved, Never to do anything, which I should be afraid to do if it were the last hour of my life.

8. Resolved, To act, in all respects, both speaking and doing, as if nobody had been so vile as I, and as if I had committed the same sins, or had the same infirmities or failings, as others; and that I will let the knowledge of their failings promote nothing but shame in myself, and prove only an occasion of my confessing my own sins and misery to God. Vid. July 30.

9. Resolved, To think much, on all occasions, of my dying, and of the common circumstances which attend death.

10. Resolved, when I feel pain, to think of the pains of martyrdom, and of hell.

11. Resolved, When I think of any theorem in divinity to be solved, immediately to do what I can towards solving it, if circumstances do not hinder.

12. Resolved, If I take delight in it as a gratification of pride, or vanity, or on any such account, immediately to throw it by.

13. Resolved, To be endeavoring to find out fit objects of liberality and charity.

14. Resolved, Never to do anything out of revenge.

15. Resolved, Never to suffer the least motions of anger towards irrational beings.

16. Resolved, Never to speak evil of any one, so that it shall tend to his dishonor, more or less, upon no account except for some real good.

17. Resolved, That I will live so, as I shall wish I had done when I come to die.

18. Resolved, To live so, at all times, as I think is best in my most devout frames, and when I have the clearest notions of the things of the gospel, and another world.

19. Resolved, Never to do anything, which I should be

afraid to do, if I expected it would not be above an hour before I should hear the last trump.

20. Resolved, To maintain the strictest temperance in eating and drinking.

21. Resolved, Never to do anything, which if I should see in another, I should count a just occasion to despise him for, or to think any way the more meanly of him.

22. Resolved, To endeavor to obtain for myself as much happiness in the other world as I possibly can, with all the power, might, vigor, and vehemence, yea violence, I am capable of, or can bring myself to exert, in any way that can be thought of.

23. Resolved, Frequently to take some deliberate action, which seems most unlikely to be done, for the glory of God, and trace it back to the original intention, designs, and ends of it; and if I find it not to be for God's glory, to repute it as a breach of the fourth Resolution.

24. Resolved, Whenever I do any conspicuously evil action, to trace it back, till I come to the original cause; and then, both carefully endeavor to do so no more, and to fight and pray with all my might against the original of it.

25. Resolved, To examine carefully and constantly, what that one thing in me is, which causes me in the least to

doubt of the love of God; and so direct all my forces against it.

26. Resolved, To cast away such things as I find do abate my assurance.

27. Resolved, Never willfully to omit anything, except the omission be for the glory of God; and frequently to examine my omissions.

28. Resolved, To study the Scriptures so steadily, constantly, and frequently, as that I may find, and plainly perceive, myself to grow in the knowledge of the same.

29. Resolved, Never to count that a prayer, nor to let that pass as a prayer, nor that as a petition of a prayer, which is so made, that I cannot hope that God will answer it; nor that as a confession which I cannot hope God will accept.

30. Resolved, To strive every week to be brought higher in religion, and to a higher exercise of grace, than I was the week before.

31. Resolved, Never to say anything at all against anybody, but when it is perfectly agreeable to the highest degree of Christian honor, and of love to mankind, agreeable to the lowest humility, and sense of my own faults and failings, and agreeable to the golden rule; often, when I have said anything against any one, to bring it to, and try it strictly by, the test of this Resolution.

32. Resolved, To be strictly and firmly faithful to my trust, that that, in Prov. xx. 6. A faithful man, who can find?' may not be partly fulfilled in me.

33. Resolved, To do always what I can towards making, maintaining, and preserving peace, when it can be done without an overbalancing detriment in other respects. Dec. 26, 1722.

34. Resolved, In narrations, never to speak anything but the pure and simple verity.

35. Resolved, Whenever I so much question whether I have done my duty, as that my quiet and calm is thereby disturbed, to set it down, and also how the question was resolved. Dec. 18, 1722.

36. Resolved, Never to speak evil of any, except I have some particular good call to it. Dec. 19, 1722.

37. Resolved, To inquire every night, as I am going to bed, wherein I have been negligent,--what sin I have committed,--and wherein I have denied myself;--also, at the end of every week, month, and year. Dec. 22 and 26, 1722.

38. Resolved, Never to utter anything that is sportive, or matter of laughter, on a Lord's day. Sabbath evening, Dec. 23, 1722.

39. Resolved, Never to do anything, of which I so much

question the lawfulness, as that I intend, at the same time, to consider and examine afterwards, whether it be lawful or not; unless I as much question the lawfulness of the omission.

40. Resolved, To inquire every night before I go to bed, whether I have acted in the best way I possibly could, with respect to eating and drinking. Jan. 7, 1723.

41. Resolved, to ask myself, at the end of every day, week, month, and year, wherein I could possibly, in any respect, have done better. Jan. 11, 1723.

42. Resolved, Frequently to renew the dedication of myself to God, which was made at my baptism, which I solemnly renewed when I was received into the communion of the church, and which I have solemnly re-made this 12th day of January, 1723.

43. Resolved, Never, henceforward, till I die, to act as if I were any way my own, but entirely and altogether God's; agreeably to what is to be found in Saturday, Jan. 12th. Jan. 12, 1723.

44. Resolved, That no other end but religion shall have any influence at all on any of my actions; and that no action shall be, in the least circumstance, any otherwise than the religious end will carry it. Jan. 12, 1723.

45. Resolved, Never to allow any pleasure or grief, joy or sorrow, nor any affection at all, nor any degree of

affection, nor any circumstance relating to it, but what helps religion. Jan. 12 and 13, 1723.

46. Resolved, Never to allow the least measure of any fretting or uneasiness at my father or mother. Resolved, to suffer no effects of it, so much as in the least alteration of speech, or motion of my eye; and to be especially careful of it with respect to any of our family.

47. Resolved, To endeavor, to my utmost, to deny whatever is not most agreeable to a good and universally sweet and benevolent, quiet, peaceable, contented and easy, compassionate and generous, humble and meek, submissive and obliging, diligent and industrious, charitable and even, patient, moderate, forgiving, and sincere, temper; and to do, at all times, what such a temper would lead me to; and to examine strictly, at the end of every week, whether I have so done. Sabbath morning, May 5, 1723.

48. Resolved, Constantly, with the utmost niceness and diligence, and the strictest scrutiny, to be looking into the state of my soul, that I may know whether I have truly an interest in Christ or not; that when I come to die, I may not have any negligence respecting this to repent of. May 26, 1723.

49. Resolved, That this never shall be, if I can help it.

50. Resolved, That I will act so, as I think I shall judge

would have been best, and most prudent, when I come into the future world. July 5, 1723.

51. Resolved, That I will act so, in every respect, as I think I shall wish I had done, if I should at last be damned. July 8, 1723.

52. I frequently hear persons in old age say how they would live, if they were to live their lives over again: Resolved, That I will live just so as I can think I shall wish I had done, supposing I live to old age. July 8, 1723.

53. Resolved, To improve every opportunity, when I am in the best and happiest frame of mind, to cast and venture my soul on the Lord Jesus Christ, to trust and confide in him, and consecrate myself wholly to him; that from this I may have assurance of my safety, knowing that I confide in my Redeemer. July 8, 1723.

54. Resolved, Whenever I hear anything spoken in commendation of any person, if I think it would be praiseworthy in me, that I will endeavor to imitate it. July 8, 1723.

55. Resolved, To endeavor, to my utmost, so to act, as I can think I should do, if I had already seen the happiness of heaven and hell torments. July 8, 1723.

56. Resolved, Never to give over, nor in the least to slacken, my fight with my corruptions, however unsuccessful I may be.

57. Resolved, When I fear misfortunes and adversity, to examine whether I have done my duty, and resolve to do it and let the event be just as Providence orders it. I will, as far as I can, be concerned about nothing but my duty and my sin. June 9, and July 13, 1723.

58. Resolved, Not only to refrain from an air of dislike, fretfulness, and anger in conversation, but to exhibit an air of love, cheerfulness, and benignity. May 27, and July 13, 1723.

59. Resolved, When I am most conscious of provocations to ill nature and anger, that I will strive most to feel and act good-naturedly; yea, at such times, to manifest good nature, though I think that in other respects it would be disadvantageous, and so as would be imprudent at other times. May 12, July 11, and July 13.

60. Resolved, Whenever my feelings begin to appear in the least out of order, when I am conscious of the least uneasiness within, or the least irregularity without, I will then subject myself to the strictest examination. July 4 and 13, 1723.

61. Resolved, That I will not give way to that listlessness which I find unbends and relaxes my mind from being fully and fixedly set on religion, whatever excuse I may have for it--that what my listlessness inclines me to do, is best to be done, &c. May 21, and July 13, 1723.

62. Resolved, Never to do anything but my duty, and then, according to Eph. vi. 6-8. to do it willingly and cheerfully, as unto the Lord, and not to man: knowing that whatever good thing any man doth, the same shall be receive of the Lord. June 25, and July 13, 1723.

63. On the supposition, that there never was to be but one individual in the world, at any one time, who was properly a complete Christian, in all respects of a right stamp, having Christianity always shining in its true lustre, and appearing excellent and lovely, from whatever part and under whatever character viewed: Resolved, To act just as I would do, if I strove with all my might to be that one, who should live in my time. Jan. 14, and July 13, 1723.

64. Resolved, When I find those "groanings which cannot be uttered," of which the apostle speaks, and those "breathings of soul for the longing it hath," of which the psalmist speaks, Psalm cxix. 20. that I will promote them to the utmost of my power; and that I will not be weary of earnestly endeavoring to vent my desires, nor of the repetitions of such earnestness. July 23, and Aug. 10, 1723.

65. Resolved, Very much to exercise myself in this, all my life long, viz. with the greatest openness of which I am capable, to declare my ways to God, and lay open my soul to him, all my sins, temptations, difficulties, sorrows, fears, hopes, desires, and every thing, and every

circumstance, according to Dr. Manton's Sermon on the 119th Psalm,. July 26, and Aug. 10, 1723.

66. Resolved, That I will endeavor always to keep a benign aspect, and air of acting and speaking, in all places, and in all companies, except it should so happen that duty requires otherwise.

67. Resolved, After afflictions, to inquire, what I am the better for them; what good I have got by them; and, what I might have got by them.

68. Resolved, To confess frankly to myself, all that which I find in myself, either infirmity or sin; and, if it be what concerns religion, also to confess the whole case to God, and implore needed help. July 23, and August 10, 1723.

69. Resolved, Always to do that, which I shall wish I had done when I see others do it. Aug. 11, 1723.

70. Let there be something of benevolence in all that I speak. Aug. 17, 1723."

Such were the excellent Resolutions formed by Jonathan Edwards at an early period of life, and which in succeeding years were regarded by him, not as unimportant records, but as containing the great principles of the spiritual life. A deep and extensive knowledge of the heart is manifest in these Resolutions, a conviction of its defects, a lively apprehension of its dangers, and an intense concern that all its tendencies should be towards God, and towards every thing required by his holy will. There is a remarkable tenderness of conscience discovered in every particular which has been stated. The man who could thus write, was not one who could easily trifle with sin, or who could enter any of its paths without the immediate reproofs of an offended conscience. This holy man trembled even at the distant view of sin; he could not willingly come near and survey its enticements. Accustomed to breathe in a holy atmosphere, the least taint of corruption immediately affected his spiritual frame. He knew no happiness except that connected with a conscience void of offence. All these rules were the suggestions of a conscience of a highly enlightened character.--They also indicate a constant sense of the presence and exact observations of the Searcher of all hearts. The writer lived as seeing him who is invisible; he set the Lord always before him; encouraging upon all occasions an earnest concern for the glory of God, the grand object for which he desired to live both upon earth and in heaven, an object compared with which all other things seemed in his view but trifles. If this were attained, all his desires were satisfied; but if this were lost or imperfectly gained, his soul was filled with anguish. These Resolutions afford ample testimony how much the author had entered into the spirit of 1 Cor. x. 31. Whether therefore ye eat, or drink, or whatsoever ye do, do all to the glory of God. They also illustrate his views of the importance of consistency of character. He was not content with accurate views of truth, or any kind of outward profession, apart from holy consistency of character. He studied, he admired, and he exhibited the influence of the gospel; a walk "worthy of the vocation wherewith he was called" was the elevated object at which he ardently aimed. He well knew that the followers of Christ are required "to hold forth the word of life," to shine as lights in the world, to instruct by their examples as well as by their words; and he desired to honor God by presenting to the view of the members of the spiritual kingdom, and also of the world, an example which might declare the reality and the beauty of religion. It is further manifest from these Resolutions, that his mind was most anxious for daily advancement in every branch of holiness. An active spiritual principle existed in him, which caused him to press forward, whatever might be the obstacles in his way. He could not be contented while one sin remained in him, while one grace was defective, or a single duty engaged in but imperfectly. He longed for the holy perfection of the heavenly world, and anticipated with joy that day when he should awake with the Divine likeness. It cannot be a matter of surprise, that with these sentiments and feelings he attained an exaltation of character seldom equaled and perhaps never surpassed.

The Resolutions which have given rise to these reflections are probably, "to persons of every age, but especially to the young, the best uninspired summary of Christian duty, the best directory to high attainment in evangelical virtue, which the mind of man has hitherto been able to form." They disclose the writer's own character, and they are admirably calculated to improve the character of every reader who fears to sin, and rejoices in the purity of the Divine will.

**The first twenty-one were written at once; as were the next ten, at a subsequent sitting. The rest were written occasionally. They are all on two detached pieces of paper.

2

Advice to Young Converts

About twenty years into his ministry, Jonathan Edwards wrote a letter to young Deborah Hatheway, a new convert in a nearby town, advising her concerning the Christian life. This letter, often reprinted during the eighteenth and nineteenth centuries, overflows with straightforward and biblically sound advice.

Dear Child,

As you desired me to send you in writing some directions on how to conduct yourself in your Christian course, I will now answer your request. The sweet remembrance of the great things I have lately seen at Suffield, and the dear affections for those persons I have conversed with there, give good evidences of a saving work of God upon their hearts and also incline me to do anything that lies in my power to contribute to the spiritual joy and prosperity of God's people there. And what I write to you, I would also say to other young women there who are your friends and companions and the children of God. Therefore, I desire you would communicate it to them as you have opportunity.

> **One** – I would advise you to keep up as great a strife and earnestness in religion in all aspects of it, as you would do if you knew yourself to be in a state of nature and you were seeking conversion. We advise persons under convictions to be extremely earnest for the kingdom of heaven, but when they have attained conversion they ought not to be the less watchful, laborious, and earnest in the whole work of religion, but the more; for they are under infinitely greater obligations. For lack of this, many persons in a few months after their conversion have begun to lose the sweet and lively sense of spiritual things, and to grow cold and flat and dark. They have pierced themselves through with many sorrows, whereas if they had done as the Apostle did in Philippians 3:12-14, their path would have been as the shining light, which shines more and more unto the perfect day. Not that I have already all this, or have already been made perfect, but I press on to take hold of that which Christ Jesus took hold of me. Brothers, I do not consider myself yet to have taken hold of it. But one thing I do: Forgetting what is behind and straining toward what is ahead, I press on toward the goal to win the prize for which God has called me heavenward in Christ Jesus. (Phil. 3:12-14)

Two – Don't slack off seeking, striving, and praying for the very same things that we exhort unconverted persons to strive for, and a degree of which you have had in conversion. Thus pray that your eyes may be opened, that you may receive your sight, that you may know your -self and be brought to God's feet, and that you may see the glory of God and Christ, may be raised from the dead, and have the love of Christ shed abroad in your heart. Those that have most of these things still need to pray for them; for there is so much blindness and hardness and pride and death remaining that they still need to have that work of God upon them, further to enlighten and enliven them. This will be a further bringing out of darkness into God's marvelous light, and a kind of new conversion and resurrection from the dead. There are very few requests that are not only proper for a natural person, but that in some sense are also proper for the godly.

Three – When you hear sermons, hear them for yourself, even though what is spoken in them may be more especially directed to the unconverted or to those that in other respects are in different circumstances from yourself. Let the chief intent of your mind be to consider what ways you can apply the things that you are hearing in the sermon. You should ask, What improvement should I make, based on these things, for my own soul's good?

Four - Though God has forgiven and forgotten your

past sins, yet don't forget them yourself. Often remember what a wretched bond slave you were in the land of Egypt. Often bring to mind your particular acts of sin before conversion, as the blessed Apostle Paul is often mentioning his old blaspheming, persecuting, and injuriousness, to the renewed humbling of his heart and acknowledging that he was the least of the apostles, and not worthy to be called an apostle, and the least of saints, and the chief of sinners. And be often in confessing your old sins to God. Also, let this following passage be often in your mind: Then, when I make atonement for all you have done, you will remember and be ashamed and never again open your mouth because of your humiliation, declares the sovereign LORD. (Ezek. 16:63).

Five - Remember that you have more cause, on some accounts a thousand times more, to lament and humble yourself for sins that have been since conversion than those that were before conversion, because of the infinitely greater obligations that are upon you to live to God. Look upon the faithfulness of Christ in unchangeably continuing his loving favor, and the unspeakable and saving fruits of his everlasting love. De, spite all your great unworthiness since your conversion, his grace remains as great or as wonderful as it was in converting you.

Six - Be always greatly humbled by your remaining sin, and never think that you lie low enough for it, but yet don't be at all discouraged or disheartened by it. Although we are exceeding sinful, we have an advocate with the Father, Jesus Christ the righteous, the preciousness of whose blood, the merit of whose righteousness, and the greatness of whose love and faithfulness infinitely overtop the highest mountains of our sins.

Seven – When you engage in the duty of prayer, come to the sacrament of the Lord's Supper, or attend any other duty of divine worship, come to Christ as Mary Magdalene did. When a woman who had lived a sinful life in that town learned that Jesus was eating at the Pharisee's house, she brought an alabaster jar of perfume, and as she stood behind him at his feet weeping, she began to wet his feet with her tears. Then she wiped them with her hair, kissed them and poured perfume on them. (Luke 7:37-38) Just like her, come and cast yourself down at his feet and kiss them, and pour forth upon him the sweet perfumed ointment of divine love, out of a pure and broken heart, as she poured her precious ointment out of her pure, alabaster, broken box.

Eight – Remember that pride is the worst viper that is in the heart, the greatest disturber of the soul's peace and sweet communion with Christ. It was the first sin that ever was, and lies lowest in the foundation of Satan's whole building. It is the most difficult to root out, and it is the most hidden, secret, and deceitful of all lust, and it often creeps in, insensibly, into the midst of religion and sometimes under the disguise of humility.

Nine - That you may pass a good judgment on your spiritual condition, always consider your best conversations and best experiences to be the ones that produce the following two effects: First, those conversations and experiences that make you least, lowest, and most like a little child; and, second, those that do most engage and fix your heart in a full and firm disposition to deny yourself for God and to spend and be spent for him.

Ten – If at any time you fall into doubts about the state of your soul under darkness and dull frames of mind, it is proper to look over past experiences. Don't, however, consume too much of your time and strength in poring and puzzling thoughts about old experiences, that in dull frames appear dim and are very much out of sight, at least as to that which is the cream and life and sweetness of them. Rather, apply yourself with all your might to an earnest pursuit after renewed experiences, new light, and new, lively acts of faith and love. One new discovery of the glory of Christ's face, and the fountain of his sweet grace and love will do more towards scattering clouds of darkness and doubting in one minute than examining old experiences by the best mark that can be given for a whole year.

Eleven – When the exercise of grace is at a low ebb, and corruption prevails, and by that means fear prevails, don't desire to have fear cast out any other way than by the reviving and prevailing of love, for it is not agreeable to the method of God's wise dispensations that it should be cast out any other way. When love is asleep, the saints need fear to restrain them from sin, and therefore it is so ordered that at such times fear comes upon them, and that more or less as love sinks. But when love is in lively exercise, persons don't need fear. The prevailing of love in the heart naturally tends to cast out fear as darkness in a room vanishes away as you let more and more of the perfect beams of the sun into it: There is no fear in love. But perfect love drives out fear, because fear has to do with punishment. The one who fears is not made perfect in love. (I John 4:18)

Twelve – You should be often exhorting and counseling and warning others, especially at such a day as this: Let us not give up meeting together, as some are in the habit of doing, but let us encourage one another and all the more as you see the Day approaching. (Heb. 10:25) And I would advise you especially to be much in exhorting children and young women who are your equals; and when you exhort others that are men, I would advise that you take opportunities for it chiefly when you are alone with them or when only young persons are present. I also want women to dress modestly, with decency and propriety, not with braided hair or gold or pearls or expensive clothes, but with good deeds, appropriate for women who profess to worship

God. A woman should learn in quietness and full submission. (1 Tim. 2:9-11)

Thirteen – When you counsel and warn others, do it earnestly, affectionately, and thoroughly. And when you are speaking to your equals, let your warnings be intermixed with expressions of your sense of your own unworthiness and of the sovereign grace that makes you differ. And, if you can with a good conscience, say how you in yourself are more unworthy than they.

Fourteen – If you would set up religious meetings of young women by yourselves, to be attended once in a while, besides the other meetings that you attend, I should think it would be very proper and profitable.

Fifteen – Under special difficulties, or when in great need of or great longings after any particular mercies for yourself or others, set apart a day of secret fasting and prayer alone. Let the day be spent not only in petitions for the mercies you desired, but in searching your heart, and looking over your past life, and confessing your sins before God, not as practiced in public prayer, but by a very particular rehearsal before God. Include the sins of your past life from your childhood up until now, both before and after conversion, with particular circumstances and aggravations. Also be very particular and as thorough as possible, spreading all the abominations of your heart before him.

Sixteen - Don't let the adversaries of religion have any grounds to say that these converts don't carry themselves any better than others. If you love those who love you, what reward will you get? Are not even the tax collectors doing that? And if you greet only your brothers, what are you doing more than others? Do not even pagans do that? Be perfect, therefore, as your heavenly Father is perfect. (Matt. 5:46-48) How holy should the children of God be! And the redeemed and the ones beloved of the Son of God should behave themselves in a manner worthy of Christ. Therefore walk as a child of the light and of the day, and adorn the doctrine of God your Savior. Particularly be much in those things that may especially be called Christian virtues, that make you like the Lamb of God. Be meek and lowly of heart and full of a pure, heavenly, and humble love to all. Abound in deeds of love to others and of self-denial for others, and let there be in you a disposition to account others better than yourself.

Seventeen – Don't talk of things of religion and matters of experience with an air of lightness and laughter, which is too much the custom in many places.

Eighteen - In all your course, walk with God and follow Christ as a little, poor, helpless child, taking hold of Christ's hand, keeping your eye on the mark of the wounds on his hands and side. From these wounds came the blood that cleanses you from sin and hides your nakedness under the skirt of the white shining robe of his righteousness.

Nineteen – Pray much for the church of God and especially that he would carry on his glorious work that he has now begun. Be much in prayer for the ministers of Christ.

Particularly I would beg a special interest in your prayers and the prayers of your Christian companions, both when you are alone and when you are together, for your affectionate friend, that rejoices over you and desires to be your servant.

In Jesus Christ,
Jonathan Edwards

ABOUT JONATHAN EDWARDS

On a cool October morning in 1703, Jonathan Edwards was born into the Connecticut home of Timothy and Esther Edwards. He grew up in a simple but vibrant Puritan community. Even as a young child, he showed a love for reading, diving into hefty theological books and learning Greek and Latin with his father's help. When he was only seven years old, he was already delving into these complex texts.

At thirteen, he started studying at Yale University, which would later become a significant part of his life. However, his path to influence wasn't straightforward. Despite his early academic successes, the years ahead would be marked by both remarkable achievements and painful setbacks. These experiences would shape his deep impact on America's philosophy and church history in the years to come.

To understand Jonathan Edwards requires delving into his deeply religious upbringing within a family esteemed for its spiritual prominence in early America. His maternal grandfather, Solomon Stoddard, held significant influence as a revered preacher in western Massachusetts for fifty years. Stoddard's powerful sermons called upon backslidden believers to return to biblical truths. Jonathan's father, Timothy, a respected congregational minister was well known for his sharp philosophical insight and fervent in theological debates.

At just twenty-three, armed with Yale education and remarkable debating skills, Jonathan Edwards took over the leadership of teh Northampton congregation his grandfather had pastored. As an optimistic young man, Edwards saw abundant opportunities ahead. He envisioned guiding souls toward spiritual enlightenment and steering churches toward a deeper understanding of truth rooted in Scripture.

Pursuing Purity and Revival Amid Societal Declension

Edwards' razor-sharp theological acumen seemed destined for a particular purpose, akin to a finely crafted instrument designed for specific tasks. This purpose heightened tensions in 1733 when rumblings of powerful spiritual awakenings rippled through New England, eventually culminating in the First Great Awakening. From his Northampton pulpit, Edwards passionately fueled these emerging revivals, becoming a leading defender and intellectual force behind the movement amid its numerous detractors.

The awakening brought tangible transformations that Edwards hoped would illuminate colonial churches dimmed by shallow spirituality and weakened commitment. Witnessing the decline in spiritual fervor, Edwards sought a revival rooted in personal experience and devout obedience, often referred to as "experimental divinity." He preached not just for intellectual understanding but for humbled hearts seeking true connection with God. By 1734, Northampton experienced its own awakening, thrusting Edwards into the limelight as a prominent spokesperson for the suddenly famous revival movement.

Amidst all the professional acclaim, Edwards remained primarily dedicated to pastoring in Northampton. Unfortunately, the fervor of the Awakening quickly escalated into bitter conflicts, leading to excessive zeal that eventually became the downfall of the revival itself.

As the fervor waned, Edwards found himself dealing with the aftermath. He worked tirelessly, tending to those who had drifted away from their renewed faith, guiding individuals grappling with emotional distress caused by the tumultuous events, and addressing the encroaching secular influences that had seeped into the community. Despite the challenges, Edwards remained committed to nurturing and restoring the spiritual well-being of his congregation.

In the early 1740s, Jonathan Edwards recognized the need to mend the cracks in the foundations of Northampton's spiritual community. He aimed to reinforce the church's membership standards, especially regarding baptism, communion, and genuine conversion. This effort clashed with a more lenient approach reminiscent of his grandfather's views, where the church welcomed even those without proven commitment to faith. Edwards, however, sought to draw clearer doctrinal and ethical boundaries, intensifying tensions further amidst growing uproar triggered by George Whitefield's controversial tour that inflamed the ongoing Awakening.

This tumultuous period culminated in Edwards' painful

dismissal from the Northampton pulpit in 1750, leaving him professionally shattered. Stripped of his status and income but unwavering in his beliefs, Edwards humbly accepted a humble missionary role among the Housatonic tribes in the frontier settlement of Stockbridge. Despite the dashed hopes, Edwards remained faithful, channeling his energies into literary pursuits and evangelism among the Native Americans.

This challenging period birthed his seminal work, "Freedom of the Human Will," a philosophical masterpiece that would later resonate across secular academia, influencing great minds like William James and Albert Einstein. Edwards' resilience and dedication during this bleak chapter in his life underscored his unwavering commitment to his convictions and his enduring impact on both religious and secular spheres.

In 1757, Edwards stepped back into the spotlight as the president of the College of New Jersey. However, tragedy struck merely months into his tenure when he succumbed to smallpox after an inoculation, leaving behind an indelible legacy. Despite the premature end of his influential life, Edwards continues to be revered for his legacy.

Centuries after his passing, institutions, fellowships, and historical accounts continue to recognize Edwards' towering significance in Colonial Christianity. His unwavering integrity and profound insights, blending mind and spirit, formed bridges between academic inquiry and lived wisdom, harmonizing America's Enlightenment ideals with its religious awakenings.

His legacy, deeply embedded in subsequent religious movements, owes much to his remarkable ability to interpret biblical texts with philosophical acumen akin to scientific observation in natural revelation. Edwards upheld the constructive role of reason in revealing God's truth, offering a strong foundation for later Christian scholars navigating secular challenges.

Additionally, Edwards shaped the core vocabulary around religious experiences for future theologians. His terms like "gracious affections" and "religious authenticity" continue to resonate in contemporary religious discussions, reflecting his adept navigation of the nuances of spiritual experiences. This pioneering insight into the contours and challenges of spiritual encounters positions Edwards as the trailblazer of American evangelicalism.

Today, Edwards' work "Freedom of the Will" remains a cornerstone in contemporary debates regarding moral agency and the interplay between Divine determinism and human responsibility. In addition, his writings continue to subtly influence Western religious discourse, shaping discussions on metaphysical concepts and ethical dimensions of human nature.

www.ingramcontent.com/pod-product-compliance
Lightning Source LLC
Chambersburg PA
CBHW050046080526
44586CB00014B/1488